It's time for a Man Plan!

Stop Kissing Frogs

Denise DeNicolo

Copyright © 2020 by Denise DeNicolo

All rights reserved. By purchase of this book, you have been licensed one copy for personal use only. No part of this publication may be reproduced, distributed or transmitted in any form or by any means, including photocopying, recording, or other electronic or mechanical methods, without the prior written permission of the copyright owner.

Stop Kissing Frogs: It's time for a Man Plan | Denise DeNicolo

ISBN-13: 978-1-7340926-3-9

Published by Brock Haus Press
www.BrockHausPress.com

Table of Contents

- **11** — Kissing Frogs
- **19** — Love At First Sight
- **27** — Values
- **33** — Baggage
- **39** — Faith
- **43** — Political Views
- **47** — Habits
- **55** — Social Interests
- **59** — Communication
- **63** — Children
- **67** — Money
- **75** — Sex
- **81** — Equality
- **89** — Do Not Touch
- **95** — Girlfriends Share
- **101** — Dating Suggestions

Dedication

This is dedicated to all women. My hope is to help you develop your Man Plan to finding Mr. Right.

Acknowledgments

I could not have done this without the loving help from the women who contributed their personal stories. Some names have been changed to protect their privacy.

Introduction

xoxo

Develop your Man Plan

Some people talk about women and marriage as if a woman's life is incomplete or unfulfilled if she doesn't get married. I disagree with that line of thinking. There are women who have no desire to get married while others may believe they just haven't found the right person yet. Either way, it is definitely possible to have companionship, experience love, and find fulfillment without a husband. An extended period of singleness can actually help you in your process of self-discovery.

A woman who feels she must get married at all costs is more prone to making choices that are motivated by fear and desperation. These choices usually compromise her standards. This is especially true when she feels her time is running out. I have heard it time and time again. "I have to be married before I'm (insert age)." Why? "I have to get married so I can have a baby." Why? Do you really have to get married to have a baby? With this mindset you are more likely to settle for someone because that's better than no man at all, but linking yourself to the wrong person is worse than being alone. There is no expiration date to finding Mr. Right. The saddest part about being in the wrong relationship is settling when you don't have to. Sometimes people don't even realize the relationship they are in is completely wrong. Being in the wrong relationship doesn't mean you're with a bad person. It simply means you're with someone who isn't right for **you**. We all have unique needs and wants and settling to be with someone who can't meet them will never turn out well.

I don't believe most women have standards that are too high. I believe the standards of some women aren't high **enough**! That said, it's important to distinguish your "must-haves" from your "nice-to-haves". A woman's list of non-negotiables should focus on the things she believes are most important. It's okay to have specific requirements.

Women become involved with Mr. Wrong because they do not have a Man Plan. Without a solid Man Plan you will date the wrong men! It's really that simple. This interactive journal is your plan to finding Mr. Right. It will help you examine your fundamental beliefs and values about relationships, love, and yourself. Develop and tailor your plan before beginning your search for the love of your life. Interview candidates. Interview lots of candidates. Then stick to the plan. If they do not measure up, move on.

This Man Plan is for your eyes only. It's your diary to finding Mr. Right. Think about how intelligent he must be. Is he college educated, self-taught, or street smart? Does he like to travel?

Does he like to read? Does he like animals and children? When you think about Mr. Right, what are you looking for? "Tall, dark, and handsome." That's the easy part of your Man Plan, knowing what you are looking for. You can't stop there. You must also consider what you are NOT looking for. It is completely normal to have desires but it makes more sense to be flexible with the things you think you can live with. Too often all your energy is focused on what you want but developing a Man Plan must also include deal breakers. If you do not have a list of deal breakers, you will stay in a relationship too long and end up with Mr. Wrong.

Think of buying property. When searching for property, you have an idea of what you want but you also know wht you don't want. If you are dead set on purchasing a one-story home, why would you look at two-story homes? You don't. Your Man Plan is no different.

An entrepreneur creates a solid business plan prior to starting a business. When building a house, the house plans are designed and then the house is built according to plan. Employers hiring to fill a vacant position in their place of business have a job description, advertise to attract applicants and then interview the most qualified candidates before selecting the most qualified person for the position. Finding Mr. Right is no different.

I encourage you to serial date rather than zeroing in on one man, settling down and becoming exclusive before you even know him. Seek out all your options. Go on many dates. Think of first dates as the beginning of a series of interviews. Interview lots of candidates. Then stick to the plan. If they do not mearure up, move on.

Be selective. Take your time. Forget about setting timelines for finding Mr. Right and getting married. You should not marry a stranger. Women marry strangers because there was courtship deception, they ignored danger signs, didn't ask enough questions, or didn't know him long enough to get all the answers. Get to know him. Ask questions.

If you're looking for a life partner, it should not matter how long it takes. Once you find Mr. Right, you have the rest of your lives together. Take your time. Get to know him. Ask questions. I'm serious! If you think I'm trying to pound this into your head, you're right!

This journal is here to help you develop your Man Plan so you make the right choice for your future life partner. But you must stick to your plan. Follow your Man Plan. Tweak your Man Plan periodically. If you don't work your Man Plan, you will settle for Mr. Wrong.

"There is no more lovely, friendly and charming relationship, communion or company than a good marriage."

~ Martin Luther King

Kissing Frogs

1

Tired of kissing frogs? You know, the ones you thought would turn into Prince Charming? By now you've probably learned there's no changing him. Let me tell you something in case you do not already know. A frog does not turn into Prince Charming. A frog is a frog. He is who he is... Mr. Wrong!

Most of us have heard the quote by Dr. Maya Angelou, "When people show you who they are, believe them the first time." There is so much truth to that sentiment. People are usually pretty clear with us about who they are, sometimes through their words but mainly through their actions. Believe that truth. When we ignore the unpleasant parts of a person, know that pain will come with that decision. Realize that your expectations won't be met and disappointment will surely follow.

The pain you experience in relationships is a result of expecting your mate to be someone other than who he truly is. We set our expectations, and even when someone shows us time and time again that he can't meet those expectations, we only end up hurt. If the man in your life shows you that he is abusive, unreliable, selfish, or any other undesirable character trait, you have to believe that's who he is. **Do not invest time and energy into a relationship based on hope.** Being hopeful is a wonderful thing, but when we continue to be hopeful in the face of facts that tell us otherwise, we are creating pain in our lives.

It's so easy to believe the good in someone, but you must also believe the bad. How bad is the bad stuff ~ the warts? Decide whether or not you can accept his warts and still remain happily involved. You need to leave if the warts bother you so deeply that staying would only result in a future of pain. Do not spend time hoping and expecting for the bad to change when it never will. Stop believing in fairy tales. A frog does not turn into Prince Charming.

Do some soul searching. There is probably a Mr. Wrong in your past, or ten Mr. Wrongs. It doesn't matter as long as you learn from them. Learn from your girlfriends' bad relationships. Throughout this journal women share their personal stories and give advice about finding your life partner, Mr. Right.

Below, list the names of frogs you've kissed. These are the guys who have made you unhappy, disappointed you, used you, abused you...

Frogs I have kissed

Frogs Have Warts

Mr. Wrong has character flaws you do not want in a life partner. These character flaws are warts. WARTS! Warts are DANGER SIGNS! Danger signs may or may not be obvious but they are there.

From the list of frogs you identified on the previous page, list below some of their warts. These are all the reasons he was Mr. Wrong. These are warts you do not want in Mr. Right.

Notice if your frogs have similarities. Do you tend to find the same types of men? Do you tend to meet them in the same settings? Is there a pattern? Identifying the similarities of the Mr. Wrongs in your life, past or present, will help you blacklist these types. Your blacklist is a list of banned or undesirable people. You will benefit from creating a blacklist to avoid those who do not have the potential of becoming your Mr. Right.

To develop a solid man plan, it is not enough to simply list all the wonderful traits of your Mr. Right and then begin your search. You must be very aware of all the danger signs of Mr. Wrong so you stay clear of that guy.

We all have met Mr. Wrong. It doesn't matter now if you only invested in him for a few minutes or several years. Don't beat yourself up over it. Learn from the past to make better choices now for your future. From today and always, you will stay away from Mr. Wrong.

Mr. Wrong has warts.

Warts are danger signs.

Always remember this!

Below, list all their common traits and identify if you see a pattern in your selection of frogs. If you do not have first-hand experience with Mr. Wrong (lucky you), think about your girlfriends' frogs.

My Frogs' Warts

Now blacklist these guys!

Why did I settle?

What I learned from my frogs

Consuela's Story

Consuela described her Mr. Wrong as rude and selfish. Her biggest issue with him was that he wouldn't let her meet anyone in his family. But he also refused to meet anyone in her family. They only spent time together when it was convenient for him. Luckily, she saw the danger signs and moved on.

Consuela was involved with a stranger. Clearly, he was hiding something and wasn't invested in their relationship. There was no way she could really know him if he did not include her in all aspects of his life. You must meet everyone in his life! Meet his family. He is a product of his environment. If his father is controlling and abusive, don't be surprised if he is too. If his mother is an alcoholic, statistics indicate that he is likely to become an alcoholic. Don't be surprised if he has a drinking problem too.

Sarah's Story

Sarah noticed that her boyfriend was reluctant to help clear the dinner dishes from the table and bring them to the kitchen. She had to remind him every time. Patrick begrudgingly did it, but only after she asked him to help. Sarah understood why Patrick was reluctant to help her with the dishes after she spent Thanksgiving with his family. When everyone was finished eating, all the men moved to the living room to watch football on television. The women were left to clear the table and clean the kitchen. Sarah was invited to help in the kitchen. All the women cleaned the kitchen while the men relaxed and watched TV.

Sarah got a preview of what life would be like if she were to marry Patrick. Patrick's family had clearly defined sex roles. It's highly unlikely that Patrick will change. Sarah will have to decide if this works for her.

Your father was the first man in your life. Was he a frog? How did he treat your mother?

What have you learned about your parents' relationship that will help you in your search for Mr. Right?

So how many frogs do you need to kiss before finding Mr. Right? It's a numbers game. The more stringent your requirements are, the fewer people there are who will meet those requirements. Be clear to yourself about what is really important. Make a list of traits and characteristics that are non-negotiable. Also ask yourself if you're being realistic.

Instead of asking yourself how many people you must kiss before finding your ideal relationship, ask yourself what is important in the relationship you are seeking. Be clear of what you want. Be clear of what you do not want. That way you are most likely to find it and you will be kissing fewer frogs.

Stick to your Man Plan. If the frog is living in the swamp jumping from lily pad to lily pad, stop kissing him.

Kelly's Story

"The first Mr. Wrong was my abusive step-father. He set the precedence for the ones that would follow. He was abusive, physically and emotionally, and would humiliate me in public. Eventually, he was sexually abusive. Those were all familiar qualities that would draw me to the men I chose."

My First Frog

My first frog was my father. Dad was the king of his castle and Mom was the housewife. "Housewife" was the job title my dad assigned her. We always ate dinner together which was when important family conversations took place. I remember one conversation in particular that has had a lasting impression on me. My mom was so excited for her friend who was attending cosmetology school that she too wanted to attend cosmetology school. This topic of conversation went on over the course of a few days. It appeared that my dad was entertaining the idea but then the conversation ended abruptly when he decided that she couldn't go to school because the family needed her at home. Mom cried with disappointment, but she never argued with his decision. I was only in the second grade at the time, but remember feeling that it was so wrong. It was that moment that I knew I would never marry a controlling man. This was my yardstick when sizing up Mr. Maybes.

Love at First Sight

2

The first thing you notice about a man is what he looks like, whether you see his picture online or you meet him in person. Even before you're set up on a blind date, you first want to know what he looks like. It takes less than one second to decide if he has a chance for your phone number. In that split second, you've determined if he's too short, too tall, too old, too young, too hairy, too bald, or too whatever. If you are not attracted to him, he's eliminated that second. He's out!

Once you've spotted Mr. Yummy, you've sized him up and found that you are drawn to his style of clothing, how he wears his hair, his smile, his voice...

What's the attraction?

Do you love tattoos or despise them?

Do you love a lean muscular build, or a plump teddy bear?

Attraction is an introduction to a relationship. It is just one factor in a relationship full of elements. We will get into other elements throughout your Man Plan; however, physical attraction is still a precursor. Let's continue with your Man Plan...

Does it matter?

Do you prefer to date someone of your race?

Do you prefer to date someone of your ethnicity?

Are you open to dating someone outside your race or ethnicity?

What are your thoughts?

What attracts you to a man?

Do you prefer to date someone close to your age?

Do you prefer to date someone younger?

Do you prefer to date someone older?

What is too young or too old?

What age range will you focus on in your search for Mr. Right?

No matter how shallow it sounds, physical attraction is important in a relationship. All it means is that you have to be attracted to the person in order for there to be sexual chemistry.

Physical attraction is the first spark to zeroing in on Mr. Right, but this is only the beginning. Mr. Yummy may not be Mr. Right. Some women will stop here and fail to explore further. This is how you settle for Mr. Wrong.

You've probably heard it from other women and you may have even said it yourself.

"But he's so good looking."

"There's so much passion between us."

Other things must outweigh physical attraction, such as companionship and emotional security, or finding your partner interesting and mentally stimulating.

"No matter how long you have been waiting, the man God has for you will surpass your expectations. You will meet him when God says so. Not a minute early, not a moment later."

~ Michelle McKinney Hammond

This takes time, a lot of time. Remember, there is no rush to finding Mr. Right. Observe and ask questions. Never assume. Take your time with Mr. Maybe. Go through the four seasons before committing to marriage. In a year you will see many sides of his personality which you may not see in just three or six months. In a budding relationship, he is on his best behavior and so are you. People can only hold their breath for so long before exposing their negative traits.

Observe your man and how he behaves around everyone in his life. His friends. His parents. His siblings. His coworkers. His ex-wife. How does he treat the waiter when you're dining out? All this matters.

I Am Attracted To

I find these men so yummy!

I'm Not Attracted To

I'm not giving these guys a chance!

Take your blinders off and look deeper. Physical attraction is not enough to sustain a relationship. If there's nothing else to keep the relationship going it's over ~ or worse, you will settle for Mr. Wrong.

List your "must haves" and "nice to haves" for Mr. Yummy. It is important to be aware of your deal breakers.

Must Haves

Nice to Haves

Deal Breakers

Alyssa's Story

Alyssa met Prince Peter at a Halloween party. This was the start of their whirlwind romance. They saw each other almost every day, if not, they talked on the phone for hours. Not a day went by without some sort of contact between the two. Alyssa joined Peter and his family on Thanksgiving and she felt right at home. They attended several holiday parties. She could not recall a time in her life when she had so much fun. It was one holiday party after another. Alyssa felt they were making history together and could see him forever in her future. Peter proposed marriage on New Years and they married on Valentine's Day. Peter was a romantic. Everything seemed perfect until they married. Once they were married, Alyssa noticed that Peter started drinking as soon as he came home from work. He was drunk every night. Prince Peter quickly became Poo-Poo Peter.

Alyssa knew Peter was a big drinker before marriage, but she passed it off as Peter just having a good time during the holidays. She ignored the danger signs, made excuses for him and married a stranger. If she had taken her time getting to know him longer, a minimum of four seasons, she may have realized he wasn't a party drinker but a problem drinker.

"When you are in a real relationship, you never have to pretend to be someone that you're not."

~ Unknown

Values

3

Your values are your yardstick in search of Mr. Right

Definition:
val·ue (valyoo) - noun

the regard that something is held to deserve; the importance, worth, or usefulness of something; a person's principles or standards of behavior; one's judgment of what is important in life

Synonyms

Principles	Ethics
Moral Code	Standards
Gain	Usefulness
Benefit	Worth
Advance	Code of Behavior

We all have values ~ traits that are considered worthwhile and represent our highest priorities and deeply held driving forces. These values are internal rules and standards that direct our lives. They guide our behavior. Make values evaluations throughout your journey to finding Mr. Right.

The most successful relationships share similar core values. Similarities set the stage for intimate relationships to develop. Individuals who appear to share similar interests and beliefs are more likely to enter into an intimate relationship.

Dissimilarity in core values will cause conflict. I have counseled troubled couples because they did not share similar core values about communication, money management, expression of emotions and other issues that affect the quality of relationships. Interpersonal similarities are needed to develop a relationship, but similar core values are needed to sustain it. Make sure your core values are compatible. The best relationships are two people dedicated to working and developing similar core values: integrity, honesty, and mutual respect.

- Integrity ~ doing the right thing when no one is looking
- Honesty ~ your word is your bond; lying is not an option
- Mutual Respect ~ treating others with respect

Differing values are either unrecognized or ignored in the beginning of most relationships because individuals believe that value differences should not be a problem for those who are deeply in love. Well, these differences can be problematic.

In Chapter 1, we covered character flaws, warts, and danger signs. Think about it. Mr. Wrong's values probably were not in harmony with your values. Now, the decision to accept someone and the role that person plays in your life is always your choice. But when you choose to have someone in your life, you have to be able to make peace with who that person is based on his actions. The more you resist that reality, the more pain you will experience.

Values form the foundation for everything that happens in our lives, especially our relationships. Whatever values you hold will inundate your relationship. If you are generally happy with your relationship, you probably selected a partner who shares similar core values. If you're unhappy in your relationship, look for dissimilarities between what you value and what your partner values. Core values inspire us to do our best to preserve the relationship and remind us of our commitment when faced with adversity.

Be mindful that no two individuals are the same, but lack of compatible core values will destroy or create distress in the relationship. If you desire to be in a healthy relationship, work to establish similar core values if they do not already exist.

The importance of values:

- If our value systems are different from others, we have conflicts in those relationships.

- If we behave in a way that is out of line with our values, we get into difficulties.

- Our values lay the foundation for our behavior in everything we do.

- Values determine how we see ourselves, how we relate to others, the goals we set, how we spend our time, and how we live.

Common interests and a good looking guy aren't enough for a lasting relationship. What you really need are the same core values. The excitement of country line dancing until you pass out will fade over time, but your shared values will remain forever. Make values evaluations a priority. It's not weird at all to get super personal and ask him invasive questions about his values. This is part of the interview process for finding Mr. Right. Continuously ask, "What core values do we share about having children, religion, finances, work ethic, and general philosophies about life?

Employers seek out employees with similar core values. They know what they want in a valued employee and they are also firm in what they do not want in their organization.

Look at this Craigslist job announcement:

> Our family owned auto repair shop for over 30 years has employment opportunities available for a Service Technician. Qualified candidates must have a minimum of five years experience and be ASE certified. We are offering top pay for an ASE certified technician that is highly skilled in electrical, air conditioning and engine performance. $1000.00 sign-on bonus possible after 90 days. This position is a leader in the shop. We expect you to help set the pace and tone while helping to develop the team around you. Collaboration and a team-first mentality are a must if you are looking for success in this role. We require review of the following to measure your fit for this role: An Associates Degree, 5+ years of strong automotive mechanical diagnosis, problem-solving and repair experience. You'll also need a high level of motivation, energy and a customer-focused attitude, valid driver's license, clean driving record and neat, clean appearance; tattoos are okay but no facial piercings. You must pass a pre-employment drug test and criminal background check. If you have a DWI conviction or currently on

Clearly, this employer's values are sprinkled throughout this job announcement. By the way, this Craigslist ad would make a great template for a Man Plan. Your Man Plan should be this thorough: list what is acceptable and what is not acceptable.

Let's not label values as "right" or "wrong". Don't waste your time getting into pissing contests about your values being right and his being wrong. The question to ask yourself is, "Do we share the same core values?"

Values Story

> Once upon a time there was a young couple in love. Together they committed several crimes of murder, kidnapping and bank robberies. They were the most famous gangster couple in history, Bonnie Parker and Clyde Barrow, known by most as "Bonnie & Clyde". Did they have values? Yes. Their values may not be yours or mine, but for Bonnie and Clyde their values were aligned. But just imagine if Amelia Earhart had hooked up with Clyde. He would have pushed up against her values and caused her outright pain.
>
> Remember, core values are not about whose values are right or wrong, but about sharing the same core values. Values are a key part of you that is so important to match with your chosen partner.

My Values

List your core values. This is your yardstick.

Make values evaluations throughout your journey!

Look at your frogs from chapter one. List their values that differed from your values.

Why were these values unrecognized or ignored?

4

Baggage

Everyone Has Baggage

You have a past. He has a past. We travel through life's journey packing and unpacking our baggage along the way. Does he have baggage that you are willing to help him unpack? Does he have baggage that are deal breakers? What baggage are you bringing to the relationship? Are you open to dating someone who has been married before? How do you feel about dating someone who has been divorced four times? Are you open to dating a man with children? If so, does it matter if he has one child or six? How do you feel about him paying child support for children from previous relationships? This could be for several years. What if his elderly parents live with him?

When you interview potential suitors, you must consider the baggage they bring to the relationship. Are you willing to accept a carry-on bag? A small suitcase? A steamer trunk?

Do you want to be married to a man who pays child support to two or three families? ~ If not, he is NOT on your Man Plan! DO NOT date him!

Do you want to be a nurse to his mentally or physically disabled brother who lives with him? If not, he is NOT on your Man Plan! DO NOT date him! In other words, if you don't mind helping him unpack his carry-on bag, don't date him if he comes along with a steamer trunk. It's that simple.

Chloe's Story

Chloe was totally disenchanted a year into her marriage. "If only I had known that his ex-wife would be at my front door exchanging their children every weekend, I would have never married him!"

Did she know he was once married when they met? Yes! Did she know he had children from a previous marriage? Yes! Chloe chose to ignore this fact would later become a problem for her. Perhaps she thought the ex-wife would disappear. If he has an ex-wife and children, the ex-wife WILL BE in his life, AND YOURS. Only you can to decide if this works for you.

Erma's Story

Erma found a wonderful man who was very loving and thoughtful. She admired that Carlos had a large family and they were very close. Erma found this an attractive quality. Not long after they were married she became resentful of Carlos and his family. The first year they were married Carlos paid for his sister's wedding. They were still recovering from that financial setback when his mother needed a new refrigerator. Carlos bought his mother a new refrigerator even though it didn't leave enough money to make their car payment that month. When his cousin and cousin's girlfriend were evicted from their apartment, Carlos offered their spare bedroom for a few weeks while they searched for another place to live. The couple lived with them for over a year. Anytime his family needed money for any reason, Carlos was there to help. He rarely was repaid. When Carlos' great-grandmother passed away, he paid for the entire funeral with no financial assistance from other family members.

There was always someone in need and Carlos was always there to rescue. Carlos and Erma did without while assisting others. Erma felt she had married his entire family. Erma knew her husband was generous and very close to his family, but she just didn't realize the extent and how this would impact their relationship. Erma probably did not ask enough questions during their courtship. Erma knew Carlos had baggage but not a trunk load.

Marianne's Story

Marianne was a sixty-four-year-old widow when she reconnected with Edgar, an old acquaintance from the early '60s. Edgar had contacted Marianne after reading her husband's obituary in the newspaper. She had some financial problems so she sold her home and moved in with Edgar. They married shortly thereafter. Trying to make his home a place she could also call home, she began redecorating with her own personal touches. Every time she tried to make changes to the home, Edgar told her to put everything back to the way it was. He wanted nothing changed from how his deceased wife had left it. Marianne couldn't even move his late wife's clothing from the dresser drawers to make room for her own belongings. She had to store her clothing in plastic storage containers, which she stacked next to the dresser. Edgar's deceased wife's dentures were in the top nightstand drawer on Marianne's side of the bed, formerly Edgar's first wife's nightstand. No, Marianne wasn't allowed to dispose of the teeth either.

Edgar had not worked through his grief and was not ready for a new wife. Marianne grew tired of living in his first wife's shadow and eventually divorced him. If he is not over a past love, DO NOT date him! DO NOT marry him! There won't be room in his heart for you.

My Baggage

List baggage you bring to relationships.

Do you have a carry-on bag, small suitcase or a trunk load?

His Baggage

What do you consider a carry-on bag?

What do you consider a suitcase?

What do you consider a trunk load?

Deal Breakers

List baggage that are your deal breakers:

> "It's okay to be a little fucked up in the head. We all are. It's only when you're fucked up in the heart that makes you a piece of shit."
>
> ~ Marilyn Monroe

Faith

5

Think about your faith. Are you spiritual? Are you religious?

Do you prefer to date someone who shares your spiritual beliefs?

Do you prefer to date someone who shares your religious beliefs?

This may or may not be important to you, but think about it. What are your thoughts?

Beliefs Mr. Right and I must share:

Beliefs that are negotiable:

If Mr. Maybe wants you to convert to his religion, what are your thoughts on this?

Can you be in a relationship with someone who practices a different religion?

Your Children

Should Mr. Right become your life partner and you have children, of what faith will your children follow? If you and Mr. Right have different spiritual or religious beliefs, what is the plan for your children's spiritual and religious upbringing?

> Women who say that sharing the same religious background is important should not make a habit of seriously entertaining guys who don't.

Deal Breakers

List deal breakers regarding your religious and spiritual beliefs:

"I look at you and see the rest of my life in front of my eyes."

~ Unknown

political views

6 Discussions about politics and what's happening in the world are important to discuss in a relationship. It shows you're paying attention to current and government affairs. Hearing another person's point of view can enlighten you on a topic that maybe you didn't have all of the facts on. Having a lively debate is healthy in a relationship, and so is having your own opinions on important issues. However, if the gap is just so wide and one person is wearing a hat that says #notmypresident and the other is wearing a red 'MAGA' hat, it's likely to be problematic. How important is this to you?

Does it matter?

Are you up on current events and feel strongly about politics?

Do you prefer to date someone with similar political views?

What political views must you share?

How important is this to you?

How will politics affect your relationship?

Deal Breakers

List deal breakers regarding your political views:

"Love is a two-way street constantly under construction."

~ Carroll Bryant

"Never marry a man you meet at a bar, or you'll marry an alcoholic like me."

~ Carl Edward Zenke

Habits

Some Habits to Consider

Bad habits may seem okay and even cute at first, but with time they can break a relationship. Do not go into a relationship thinking that you will break his bad habits. Remember, kissing a frog doesn't turn him into Prince Charming.

How do you feel about smoking or chewing tobacco? How do you feel about the toilet seat being left up? Table manners? Picking his nose and farting in public? Think of all the possible habits.

We all have habits, good and bad. You really need to think about what habits are deal breakers. His annoying habits may slap you in the face on a daily basis. If he talks and laughs with food in his mouth and ends up wearing his meal on his shirt, how long do you think you can tolerate this if this sort of thing bothers you? Should you eliminate him after the first date or a year later?

Remember, you can't go into this believing it will get better or you can change him. Accept him for who he is and not who you want him to become.

Good Habits Important to Me

Bad Habits I Despise

Use of Substances

When you were a little girl, did you ever say, "When I grow up I want to marry an alcoholic?" Probably not. So why would you knowingly marry an alcoholic? Because you ignored the signs or made excuses for him. When we ignore the unpleasant parts of a person, know that pain will come with that decision. Believe that truth.

Here are some questions to consider on your quest for finding Mr. Right:

How do you feel about drinking alcohol socially? Drinking alcohol excessively? What about smoking marijuana? Using cocaine or heroin? Does he cook his own crystal meth? Does he sell drugs or do his friends sell drugs? Does he take prescription medication not prescribed to him? Does he overuse his prescription medication?

Has he ever been arrested for drug or alcohol related crimes? Does he have to report to a probation officer?

Too often women say, "I didn't know he had a problem." They did know! All the signs were right in front of them. They found explanations or they simply ignored the signs altogether. The clues were there! They are always there!

Decide if substance use is an issue. Some women do not have a problem with it. Take, for example, Miss Plenty-Of-Fish who stated in the first sentence of her dating profile "Share Your Drugs". And then there is Miss Zoosk who described herself, "I smoke. I smoke a lot. I drink. I drink a lot. I party. I party a lot. Not looking for someone who is judgmental". Miss Plenty-Of-Fish and Miss Zoosk are clear about who they are trying to attract.

Only you can decide if his substance use is an issue.

If your man has an addiction and isn't in recovery, you cannot be his therapist. You cannot reform him. He has to do that on his own at his own free will. Substance use is a major problem in relationships. It destroys them. This is something to consider when developing your Man Plan. If you do not share the same values regarding addictions, whether it's alcohol, drugs, gambling or sex, there will be conflict. Make values evaluations.

"True love stories never have endings."

~ Richard Bach

Lois' Story

Lois recently started dating a man through work she's known for a couple of years. Vincent is courteous, kind, and a lot of fun to be around. They always have a good time together. Lois has noticed that Vincent can drink large amounts of alcohol without getting drunk. Because she has never seen him drunk she doesn't think he is an alcoholic, or that he even has a problem. Vincent has a pending Class A Misdemeanor charge for a DWI. So far Lois believes his DWI is an isolated incident, just bad luck. Lois is hopeful that Vincent is her Mr. Right.

If you were dating Vincent, would you think he has a drinking problem? Vincent can drink large amounts of alcohol because he's had plenty of practice. It's called a "high tolerance". Lois is focused on all his good qualities and ignoring the danger signs.

Remember how we can decide in a split second if we are attracted to someone or not? If there is no immediate attraction, we will eliminate him in that split second. So why does it take so much (much, much, much) longer to eliminate him when the danger signs are flashing right in front of you? Think about that throughout your journey to finding Mr. Right.

When dangers signs are flashing, know when to eliminate him. Don't wait for him to change. Don't believe it will get better. Knowing when to eliminate him is important.

Signs He May Have An Addiction

Social Interests

8

My Social Interests

We gravitate towards those who share common hobbies and interests.

Attraction is a great start when finding Mr. Right, but social interests you both share keep the relationship going. That's only if you share core values. Remember, values come first, then common interests.

List some of your hobbies and interests you would enjoy doing together with Mr. Right. Also list social interests that you do not find appealing.

What I like to do:

What I don't like to do:

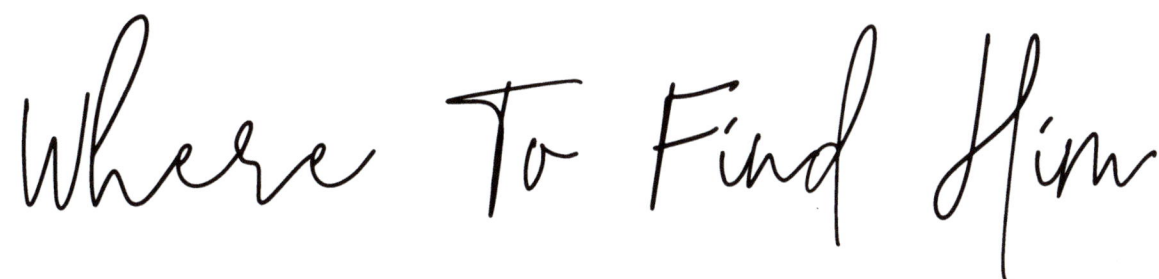

Where To Find Him

Think about your social interests. This is where you start your search for Mr. Right.

When you're online searching for a potential date, read his profile carefully. What does he say he likes to do? Does he mention what he does not like? Does he describe you as his desired woman?

When you're doing whatever you enjoy doing, look around for Mr. Right, whether it's at a 5K fun run or at an art museum. If you don't want a party boy, don't look for dates at a bar.

Look within the circles you travel. Your friends have friends. Let them know you are available and looking. Make connections through work. Single men are everywhere!

Solitude may even enhance relations making time together more valuable. So don't feel you have to do everything together all the time. Having some different interests can keep the relationship interesting.

Places I can look for him:

"A relationship between a husband and wife should be one of closest friends."

~ B. R. Ambedkar

9 Communication

Are you looking for a partner who is thought provoking, intellectual and a stimulating conversationalist?

How he communicates is usually obvious on the first date.

Does he know what he doesn't know? Is he curious in learning more of what he doesn't know?

Or does he already know everything, even better than you?

Does he try to one-up you or others?

Does he interrupt you or others?

When others ask you questions, does he answer for you?

Does he call you names or tell you that you are stupid?

How does he speak to others?

Do you prefer the quiet ones who are good listeners?

How he communicates is more important than you may think.

Let's examine some communication styles and how they work. Although we all use different communication styles in different situations, we each have a favored style we use the most. While you read about the following styles, think about your own. Pay attention to how your dates communicate.

AGGRESSIVE: Expressing yourself with an attitude of intimidation: little regard for others' rights, thoughts, or feelings. Aggressive communication can be abusive, threatening, and judgmental and may include name-calling, yelling, interrupting, sarcasm, ridicule, and hostile body language.

PASSIVE-AGGRESSIVE: Not expressing yourself openly, but instead hinting, being indirect, or being silent about what you want, think, or feel; talking behind others' backs; being sarcastic; pouting; whining; constant complaining; expecting others to know what you think, feel, or want without telling them; refusing to talk even though you're visibly upset.

PASSIVE: Not feeling you have a right to feelings or opinions or the right to express yourself in any way that might upset others, or possibly any way at all; giving short, uninformative answers; agreeing with whatever others say.

ASSERTIVE: Expressing your thoughts, feelings, and wishes without ignoring those of others; being able to disagree openly and say "no" in a way that respects both others and yourself.

MIND READING: This means describing what you believe the other person thinks and feels or what you think his or her reasons are for things he or she did. You might be right, but you might be misunderstanding or there might be factors you don't know. Most of us get angry or frustrated when others try to tell us what we think or feel, and this often triggers arguments or angry outbursts. Usually when we mind-read we are not really trying to communicate. We are trying to dominate and control the other person, and no one wants to be dominated or controlled. Think about the last time someone read your mind in a conversation with you.

NAME-CALLING: Usually when we are upset with people it is because of something they did or did not do; in other words, their actions. Calling people names is not referring to their actions. It is labeling them. This is frustrating for them, because they may be able to change their actions, but they can't change who and what they are. When we call them names, we're telling them that this thing they can't change – who and what they are – is wrong or unacceptable. Besides this, name-calling is one of the most proven ways known to trigger anger in someone else and turn a discussion into an argument or a fight. Usually when we call people names, we are not trying to communicate. We are expressing anger and aggression, and the natural reaction on their part is to become defensive and counterattack.

INTERRUPTING / LONG SPEECHES: These two guidelines go together. When we cut others off (including finishing their sentences for them), the message we are giving them is, "What you have to say is not important enough for any more of my time. Shut up! What I have to say is more important than your thoughts or feelings." Of course, for us to be willing to let the other person talk uninterrupted, we have to know that we will have a chance to express ourselves too. So if we want others to stop interrupting us, we have to give them their time to talk also, and if we monopolize the conversation with long-winded speeches we are denying them that time. Both interrupting and making long speeches are often ways to control others rather than ways to communicate effectively. Again, none of us like to be controlled by others.

My communication style:

Deal Breakers

List deal breakers regarding how he communicates:

"If you love someone, set them free. If they come back they're yours. If they don't, they never were."

~~ Richard Bach

10 Children

Do you plan to have children?

Are you open to adoption?

Do you have children from a previous relationship?

If a man tells you he does not want children, or if he already has children and tells you he does not want more, believe him. You can't kiss him until he changes his mind.

Melanie's Story

Melanie married when she was 19 years old. Her husband told her all along that he was not interested in having children. Melanie was hopeful he would change his mind. He didn't. By the time she was 28 years old, she finally realized he was not giving in. Having children was very important to her, so Melanie "accidentally" got pregnant. Things got ugly. Her husband forced her to have an abortion; ultimately, they divorced.

Melanie and her husband had different values about marriage and family. She invested time and energy into this relationship based on hope and ignored the facts. Melanie's husband never misled her.

Jo Ann's Story

Jo Ann always wanted three children. When she and Dexter discussed marriage and family, Dexter agreed to have one child, but not three. Dexter already had two children from a previous marriage. Jo Ann insisted on having three children. Dexter never gave in; he only agreed to one child. Neither Dexter nor Jo Ann would budge. Jo Ann decided to end the relationship and began her search for Mr. Right who also wanted three children. Jo Ann found him, but they could not conceive. Jo Ann always felt that Dexter was the love of her life and regrets that she ended the relationship.

Was Jo Ann too rigid with her must-haves or was this a deal breaker and she knew she had to eliminate him? Sometimes the decision is not that simple.

If you have children from a previous relationship, what role do you expect he will play in terms of supervision, discipline, support and protection?

"A loving relationship is one in which the loved one is free to be himself: to laugh with me, but never at me; to cry with me, but never because of me; to love life, to love himself, to love being loved. Such a relationship is based upon freedom and can never grow in a jealous heart."

~ Leo F. Buscaglia

Money

*What does money mean to you?
Are you a saver or a spender?*

A woman who knows that financial stability is important should eliminate potential suitors whose actions show they can't be trusted with money.

In this chapter, we will look at money, how you value money and how he values money. Are you financially compatible? Some people may have no problem with money individually; the trouble starts after they're in a relationship and discover they are money-minded opposites.

Couples frequently avoid talking about money before marriage. Sharing perspectives about money can help couples resolve the financial issues that doom many marriages. It's important that you don't interrogate him prematurely about his finances, but before you get to that point in your relationship when it's appropriate to talk about money matters ~ observe, observe, observe.

Observe how he manages his money. Is his car payment more than the rent on his apartment? Does he like to buy big toys, but always scrimping to make ends meet? Is he financially supporting extended family members?

Does he have investments? Is he frugal, being economical, prudently saving and sparing and not wasteful? Or is he such tightwad that he washes out his Ziploc® sandwich bags for reuse?

Are you financial compatibles or money-minded opposites? Remember your values evaluations and look for danger signs.

It's inappropriate to ask financial questions at the beginning of the relationship. Talk finances when the relationship is serious and you're talking about living together or getting married.

Same Story, Different Frogs

I was widowed at twenty-four. Once I started dating again, I had several first and second dates with men who asked me about my husband's life insurance policy. Each time my inside voice asked, "No. Did he really just ask me that?" All I could see in front of me were red flashing lights. I followed my gut and eliminated these guys immediately.

Alejandra's Story

Alejandra had inherited her grandmother's property and life savings. She felt financially secure for the first time in her life. A few men wanted a piece of her pie. They soon came out of the swamp after her grandmother passed away. Alejandra was looking for love and never thought someone would want her just for her money. Sadly, she married Mr. Wrong after a short courtship of four months. Before their first anniversary Alejandra had paid $23,000 toward his credit card debt and he still had over $100,000 in student loans, which she was helping him pay off. In the meantime, she bought him a new BMW and a motorcycle. Mr. Wrong was three years behind on his child support so she was helping him get up to date on that as well. His money problems never seemed to end. Alejandra realized that she and Mr. Wrong had different values regarding money, but she did not see this before they married. Now Alejandra feels stuck in this marriage because she has invested so much money. She believes that if she had dated him longer she would have seen the danger signs.

How much money do you expect Mr. Right to earn?

Is it important that he earns more money than you?

How do you feel about a man who earns less money than you?

Justine's Story

Justine dated Jason for about two months when they started talking about marriage. They agreed to live together and have a long engagement. Justine was very particular about her engagement ring, so they went to the jeweler's together to pick it out. Jason's credit card was declined so Justine paid for her ring. This wasn't a problem for Justine. After all, they were going to pool their money and live happily ever after. Right? Once they lived together, she discovered he had no money for anything. Most of his money was going to two families for child support. Jason also bought his five children clothing and toys in addition to the child support he paid their mothers. He had outstanding balances on all his accounts for his big boy toys: new Mercedes, sailboat (and marina storage fees), motorcycle, riding lawnmower, impressive theater room with all the works, and the list continued. Soon Justine was paying on all those accounts in an effort to be debit free which she highly valued. As soon as one debt was paid, Jason had a new debt. He just couldn't help himself. Justine finally realized that she and Jason were money-minded opposites. They did not live happily ever after.

Whatever his financial situation is, accept that's how he values money matters. If his money management is scary, especially if his credit cards are maxed out, do not think for one moment that you can help teach him to be more responsible once you're married. Marriage doesn't turn problems into miracles. Pay attention to danger signs!

What does he want to know about your finances?

His Debt

Are you okay with a man who has debt?

How do you feel about his debt?

What do you consider too much debt?

If he has more debt than you think is necessary, what are your thoughts about helping him him pay off his debt?

My Debt

Do you have debt?

How do you feel about your own debt?

What do you consider too much debt for yourself?

What is your FICO (credit) score?

Do you expect him to help you pay off your debt?

How do you expect you, as a couple, will manage your finances?

Sharing Finances

Do you plan to share your money with Mr. Right?

Do you plan to have separate bank accounts?

Do you plan to have joint bank accounts?

Do you plan to share your income?

Do you expect Mr. Right to tell you about all his income, expenses, and investments?

My ideal fiances with Mr. Right:

Mr. Right may have his own ideas about finances, which may differ from yours. This is an area that requires lots of communication and compromise for the life of your relationship.

What are your beliefs about prenuptial agreements? Would you sign one or ask Mr. Right to sign one?

are you financial compatibles or money-minded opposites?

Questions to Ask Myself

Will sex wait until marriage? Is sex before marriage okay for you? When is it okay to have sex with a new partner?

Sex tends to emotionally bond you in a relationship. Timing is important. Sex too soon can mean becoming emotionally involved with Mr. Wrong.

In Steve Harvey's book, *Act Like A Lady Think Like A Man*, the author suggests putting men on a 90-day probation period ~ no sex. During the 90 days, you should be checking him out – does he come when he says he's going to come; does he call when he's going to be late; does he like and care about your friends and, if you have children, does he express his joy at being in their presence? This gives women a chance to learn the person they are dating without the distraction of sex.

Steve compares having sex for the first time with a man you are dating to work benefits. He says that if you have to be employed with a company for 90 days before getting the benefits why should relationships be any different?

Everyone is different. What's right for one woman, may not be right for another. Remember, this is about finding Mr. Right and not becoming emotionally involved with Mr. Wrong ~ or worse, keeping Mr. Wrong for too long.

What's your sex rule? Do you have a 30-day, 60-day, 90-day rule? If you don't have a sex rule, get one.

30-Day Rule: Be honest. How well do you know someone in 30 days? This is usually the time you idealize him. He may seem like Mr. Right when he just might be Mr. Wrong. Sex too soon clutters the mind.

60-Day Rule: By now you know him better. This is when some of his flaws surface and you decide if they are deal breakers or not.

90-Day Rule: You have some pretty high standards and you are worth the wait for Mr. Right. Mr. Wrong won't wait this long because all he wanted in the first place was to get into your panties.

There are players out there who are just looking for an easy hook up, but there are also Prince Charmings. Remember this is about finding Mr. Right and not becoming emotionally involved with Mr. Wrong.

Shelly's Story

"I dated a guy for several months in my early 20s. I was very upfront that I planned on waiting to have sex until I was married. This became almost a challenge for Mr. Wrong. It seemed that every date was geared to finish with the hopes of sleeping with me. I finally ended the relationship and told him he didn't value me or my beliefs. I thought by sharing my concerns and desires to remain a virgin until marriage that he would respect this. It instead inspired some twisted game for him to try and figure different ways to lure me in. If you don't see the person respects you enough to honor you, get out!"

My Sex Rules

Every woman should have sex rules!

Deal Breakers

List deal breakers regarding your sex rules:

> *"If you find Mr. Right but don't have sexual compatibility, it's not right!"*
>
> ~ Tiffany

Tiffany's Advice

Tiffany believes you should have premarital sex to find out if you're sexually compatible. In other words, "try on the shoes before you buy them". If you're thinking about England during sex, then there is a problem. If you're not sexually compatible, then you need to seek help from a professional; otherwise, you'll be unhappy. Tiffany encourages women to give compliments to their men because she doesn't believe women do this frequently enough. "Men need compliments too!" She encourages you to say things like "you're hot" and "your ass is amazing".

Equality

13

When you were a little girl, did you ever say, "When I grow up I want to marry someone who disrespects me and abuses me?" Probably not! So why would you knowingly marry an abusive person? Because you ignored the signs or believed his excuses for his bad behavior.

We all should be with someone who treats us with the love, respect and the support we deserve. Anything less means we've chosen the wrong person. Many, many, many women have come to me for therapy because they are in abusive relationships. The danger signs usually creep up gradually and progressively get worse. It RARELY gets better. As soon as those danger signs pop up EXIT the relationship. "But I love him!" Being in love is not enough to justify staying with someone. Being in love doesn't necessarily mean you are in the right relationship. Love is not enough. We all need more than love to sustain a healthy, long-lasting relationship, the right relationship.

In this chapter, we will look at the eight elements of a healthy relationship and the eight elements of an unhealthy relationship.

Elements of Equality

A healthy relationship is a partnership, not ownership. You don't own him and he doesn't own you. A partnership is just that, two people working together in a healthy relationship ~ two equals. It's really that simple.

Let's look at the eight elements of equality, a healthy relationship.

Element #1 - Non-Threatening Behavior

- Talking and acting in a non-threatening manner, so that each feels safe and comfortable expressing oneself and doing things independently

Element #2 - Respect

- Listening to your partner non-judgmentally

- Being emotionally affirming and understanding

- Valuing each other's opinions

Element #3 - Trust & Support

- Supporting one another's goals in life

- Respecting your partner's right to own his or her feelings, friends, activities and opinions

Element #4 - Honesty & Accountability

- Accepting responsibility for oneself

- Acknowledging past use of violence

- Admitting being wrong

- Communicating opening and truthfully

Element #5 – Responsible Parenting

- Sharing parental responsibilities
- Being a positive, non-violent role model for the children

Element #6 – Shared Responsibility

- Mutually agreeing on a fair distribution of work
- Making family decisions together

Element #7 – Economic Partnership

- Making money decisions together
- Making sure both partners benefit from financial arrangements

Element #8 – Negotiation & Fairness

- Seeking mutually satisfying resolutions to conflict
- Accepting changes
- Being willing to compromise

Elements of Power & Control

In an unhealthy relationship, there is inequality, a misuse of power and control of one person over the other. This is not a partnership. One person feels a sense of power and control over the other ~ ownership.

Let's look at the eight elements of power and control.

Element #1 – Intimidation

- Making one feel afraid by using looks, actions, and gestures
- Smashing things
- Destroying one's property
- Abusing pets
- Displaying weapons

Element #2 – Emotional Abuse

- Putting one down
- Making the person feel bad about oneself
- Name-calling
- Playing mind games
- Humiliation

Element #3 – Isolation

- Controlling what the other does, whom s/he sees and talks to, and needing to know their whereabouts
- Limiting outside involvement
- Alienating you from those you love
- Using jealousy to justify actions

Element #4 – Minimizing, Denying, Blaming

- Making light of the abuse and not taking one's concerns about it seriously
- Saying the abuse didn't happen
- Shifting responsibility for abusive behavior or saying the other caused it

Element #5 – Using Children

- Making one feel guilty about the children
- Using the children to relay messages
- Using visitation as harassment
- Threatening to take the children away

Element #6 – Economic Abuse

- Preventing one from getting or keeping a job
- Making one ask for money
- Giving an allowance
- Not letting partner know about or have access to family income

Element #7 - Male privilege

- He treats her like a servant: making all the big decisions, acting like the "king of his castle".
- He has clearly defined sex roles for men and women which he expects you to follow.

Element #8 - Coercion & Threats

- Making and carrying out threats to hurt the other person
- Making threats to leave the relationship, commit suicide, or report to authorities
- Making the person do illegal things

List Unhealthy Elements of Past Relationships

Melissa's Story

Melissa married her first boyfriend. She and Sven worked the night shift at Amazon for about a year before they began dating and married shortly thereafter. Sven was very loving and attentive. Melissa and Sven rode to work together; therefore, they only needed one vehicle. Melissa loved being with Sven and Sven loved being with Melissa. They went to work together. They went to the grocery store together. They ran all their errands together. One car. One happy couple. Since they were always together, they also shared one cell phone. No reason to pay for a second phone since they were always together. Not only did they share one vehicle and one phone, they shared one wallet and one wristwatch. Sven thought this was most economical. Problems started when Melissa wanted to visit her family out of state and Sven couldn't get the time off from work to go with her. Sven did not allow Melissa to visit her family without him because it wasn't safe for her to travel alone. Melissa wasn't allowed to go anywhere without Sven, not to the grocery store, not to a medical appointment, nowhere. Melissa wasn't allowed to communicate with her family or have friends. According to Sven, he was her family and her best friend. Melissa moved to day shift, so they had to purchase another vehicle. They continued sharing the phone, the wallet and the watch, which were exchanged at shift change, so whoever was at work would have them. Sven grew suspicious of Melissa while she was at work. After all, she had a vehicle, the wallet, and the phone to do whatever she wanted without his knowledge. He grew jealous and accusatory. Everyday Sven interrogated her about looking at or talking to male coworkers. It took Melissa ten years to realize she was in a controlling relationship. Her move to day shift was her wake-up call. She finally reached her limit and filed for divorce.

"Jealousy is indeed a poor medium to secure love, but it is a secure medium to destroy one's self-respect."

— Emma Goodman

Do not touch

14

Mr. Wrong wears a danger sign, but the sign may be invisible if you are blinded by passion. Open your eyes. Read the small print. Do not make excuses for him or ignore clues. Eliminate anyone with a danger sign stamped on his forehead. No one is perfect. Everyone has flaws, including you. Danger signs are flaws you cannot live with so understand that a life with a man wearing a danger sign will bring you pain. Only you can decide the flaws you are willing to accept in a life partner. Look for clues on your first date. Some danger signs become clearer with time, but get the hell out of there as soon as you catch on.

It is important to know what you do not want in a man when developing your Man Plan. This makes the journey easier than only focusing on what you do want. Develop your Man Plan and stick to it. You may have to tweak it over time. Tweaking your plan just means you are getting better with realistic expectations and being more selective.

Once you dump Mr. Wrong, move on and continue your search for Mr. Right.

Danger signs are warning signs in relationships. Take a look at some points to consider. These are indications that you may not have found Mr. Right.

- If most of your time consists of disagreements and arguments that never get resolved, marriage will make them worse.

- If he treats you like he is your parent, ask yourself if this works for you in the long haul.

- He supports all your interests and activities but then reacts to you engaging in them. This will not get better with time.

- Don't marry because the sex is wonderful. Physical intimacy won't keep the marriage going by itself. You also need emotional, social, spiritual, intellectual and recreational intimacy.

- If either of you has not recovered from a previous relationship, you're not ready for this one.

- If he has an addiction and is not in recovery, you cannot be his therapist. Do not live on hope based on promises.

- If he or you is asking, "Are you really in love with me", this is an indication of uncertainty and/or low self-esteem.

- You have a beloved pet and he does not like animals. Ask yourself which you should eliminate, your beloved pet or him.

Through my journey writing this journal several women have shared their personal experiences to help you with your Man Plan. Many of their stories have similarities. You may identify with them. You may have to kiss many frogs before finding Mr. Right.

The following three pages is the Frog Alert Checklist which you might find helpful. This is a screening tool.

Use this FROG ALERT CHECKLIST to assess each of your Mr. Maybes.

Frog Alert Checklist

Use this checklist to identify possible danger signs that he is Mr. Wrong.

His Name: _____   His Score: _____

I. Projecting the Future

- [ ] Would I want to spend the rest of my life with him, exactly as he is?
- [ ] Would I want this man to raise my children?
- [ ] Would I want my children to be exactly like him?

II. Am I Talking Myself into this Relationship?

- [ ] I am talking myself into this relationship.
- [ ] His status or appearance builds my self-esteem.
- [ ] We have some things in common but I'm avoiding looking at some obvious differences.
- [ ] I'm focusing on one important quality (sex, money, status, etc.) and ignoring unmet requirements.
- [ ] I see that he has so much potential. I can help him.
- [ ] We have different values.

_____ # CHECKS IN SECTION II

III. Danger Signs I Might Be Ignoring

- Blames others for his life choices and circumstances
- Tries controlling everything, including me
- Immature, impulsive, irresponsible
- Emotionally distant, aloof
- Still pining for a past relationship
- Married or unavailable
- Lacks integrity when dealing with others or money
- Is pessimistic or negative about things that matter to me
- Judgmental attitude towards me or others
- Active addiction, addictive behavior (rationalized as "not a problem")
- Emotional roller coaster, recurring or regular emotional drama
- Overly quiet or withdrawn
- Talks too much, especially about himself, monopolizes conversations
- I am trying to change him to fit what I want, instead of accepting him for who he is.
- Doesn't listen
- Inconsistent and changeable behavior
- This is not what I want but I don't want to be alone.
- What he says about himself doesn't match reality.
- Unwilling to self-examine, accept feedback, or take responsibility
- Doesn't keep promises or agreements

CHECKS IN SECTION III

IV. Results

Total all checks from sections II and III: ▢

Circle each item you checked that you consider the biggest problems.

On a scale of 0 (not at all) to 10 (perfect) my minimum score for a relationship is: ▢

On a scale of 0 (not at all) to 10 (perfect) I score this Mr. Maybe: ▢

Based on these results, Mr. Maybe is:

▢ Mr. Right

▢ Mr. Wrong (now is the time to eliminate him)

15 Girlfriends Share

He's married. There's no future with a married man. If he doesn't tell you he's married, the signs are still there. He doesn't spend holidays (or weekends) with you, you haven't met his kids, he won't "friend" you on Facebook, and you've never been to his home. If he's upfront about being married, he has creative explanations about being unfaithful to his wife. Don't fool yourself into believing that he is with you because you are so super terrific. If he leaves his wife for you, he will cheat on you too. He's a cheater.

You can spot him on your first date. He's impressive! He tells you how wonderful he is, what he owns, and all that he has achieved. He exaggerates. He doesn't seem interested in knowing anything about you, because he is there to sell himself to you. He's proud and perfect. Don't get involved. You'll never measure up and you will drive yourself nuts trying to please him. You will never come first. He will.

He has an addiction. It doesn't matter if it's alcohol, cocaine, gambling or sex. The addiction will always come first. Don't stick around to take care of him, bail him out of jail, or wait for him to clean up his act. Addicts are liars and they are very good at it. He's not too difficult to spot. He'll use his addiction to sulk or celebrate. The addiction will dominate and destroy your life.

He can't hold a job. He is either frequently changing jobs or fired. There are always really good reasons too. You'll find he is unreliable. You can't count on him for anything. If he can't keep a job, he won't contribute financially or help take care of the kids. You will be his parent.

First, he's jealous. It's all your fault. Then he will use his power to control you. He needs to know your whereabouts at all times, and he doesn't like your friends or family. He will dictate how you wear your hair and the clothes you wear. You have no voice. He owns you. You are his possession. Get out at the first clue because it will just get worse.

"If your instincts are telling you that something is not right, listen to it! Don't believe that you are going to change him or he will change you! If he lays his hands on you one time, it's one time too many!" ~ Evelyn

"Anything that seems to be a red flag in the beginning is usually going to be the demise of the relationship. People don't change. He's not going to be more thoughtful and you aren't going to learn to live with less." ~ Susan

"Listen to your gut." Deb had suspicions that Mr. Wrong was cheating on her. She and Mr. Wrong owned a business together. She advises that if you work with your man, be sure to work extra hard on having fun together. "If a man has a temper or issues with violence, even once, get away. It never gets better, only worse." ~ Deb

"Please never believe that you can fix them. Never believe you're the one who needs fixing. Muster up the courage and just get out." ~ Kim

"Don't settle for someone because you think that's the only person that can love you. Value yourself! You deserve the best! Be sure to have common principles and moral values with that person before establishing a commitment." ~ Anonymous

"Get out as quickly as you realize you are with a Peter Pan who doesn't respect you." ~ Annie

"If a guy isn't the one making the effort, cut your losses and move on. I wish I wouldn't have wasted so much time on someone who clearly wasn't that into me." ~ Linda

"I would advise women to get their resume. Know their employment background, their credit history and learn about their past relationships (why they ended and who ended it). Be upfront about what you are looking for in a relationship." ~ Debbie

"Pay attention to your inner feeling. A lot of times a guy looks perfect but you have to have things in common. Have a good time together without forcing anything. Have the same values and views in life or at least similar. Do not settle. Don't have preconceived ideas and trust your gut." ~ Jimena

"Give the relationship plenty of time before getting married. If you see any signs of abusive behavior, run immediately! If you get a gut feeling about anything, trust your instincts. If they tell you to get out of the relationship, just do it. There is someone better waiting." ~ Olivia

Pepper was in a relationship with Mr. Wrong for two years. She described him as egotistical, controlling, physically abusive and was irrationally suspicious and jealous. Her Mr. Wrong masked it all with his charm. Pepper advises to trust your first gut instincts. They are there to protect you. Break all ties at the first sign of abusive behavior. Fortunately, Pepper trusted her instincts and left the relationship. She found her Mr. Right and has been married for 32 years. She and her Mr. Right share the same values, faith, political leanings and both come from families with stable, lengthy marriages. Her Mr. Right is financially responsible, affectionate and adventurous. They have similar interests in fitness and leisure activities.

Deb had specific criterion for her Mr. Right. He had to be employed, own a car and have a definite plan for the future. We can surmise that Deb probably had her share of the unemployed with no goals.

"I have a diary that says, 'I met an interesting man at lunch today. He looks like trouble.' He was." ~ Ellen

Suzette's Story

Suzette met Lamar on Tinder, a dating app. She quickly fell in love with Lamar. She knew he was her future husband within the first month of courtship. But Lamar still played on Tinder. Suzette put all her love and energy into this relationship and wanted to prove to Lamar that she would be the perfect wife. While Lamar was at work, she would go to his house to surprise him by doing his laundry, cleaning his house and having dinner ready when he walked through the door. For their two-month anniversary Suzette prepared a special dinner by candle light, expecting him to walk through the door at 6 o'clock. But Lamar didn't come home until 9 o'clock because he had dinner with his mother instead. Suzette was heartbroken. Lamar broke off their relationship a few weeks later. Suzette was devastated but did not give up. In her mind, he was her future husband. With Suzette's persistence they reconciled. Lamar continued making plans that did not include her, while Suzette increased her effort to prove that she would be the perfect wife. Lamar continued to play on Tinder. When Suzette had health problems that required immediate medical attention, Lamar dropped her off at the emergency room. He didn't want to wait around, and told her to call him when she was done. Suzette called Lamar when she was ready to be picked up. She called several times before he answered. Lamar denied that he had promised to pick her up; he simply told her to call him when she was done. Suzette's only other ride was her mother who lived 80 miles away. Again, Suzette was heartbroken.

Even though Lamar remained uncommitted, Suzette was hopeful that Lamar would marry her.

Poor Suzette put all her eggs in one basket and ignored the warning signs that Lamar just wasn't into her. Suzette was living on hope which is not a wonderful thing in this case.

Mariah's Story

"He was dishonest from the very onset. Little white lies here and there. He was charming and paid attention to me; it didn't take much. He didn't flinch when I told him I had two-year-old twin daughters. When I introduced him to my daughters, he was sweet and very natural being around children, and in the back of my mind I wanted a stable father figure for them. He welcomed the task. Over the years he wasn't a philanderer, wasn't a pervert, wasn't (consistently) physically abusive, but his abuse was just below the surface and much harder to detect; it was psychological and manipulative and intentional. He played on my own sense of goodness and morality, and on my desire to keep my family intact. And for 15 years I unknowingly played into his con. Ultimately, it ended because of his refusal to tell the truth. Even when I fact-checked his stories and exposed his lies, he still denied reality. The lies were hugely about his drinking for the middle years of our marriage, but even after rehab he showed no real conscience about a single lie. He was always calm and (seemingly) rational as he attempted to distort my perception of reality every single day."

Another One of My Frogs

Anyone who knows me knows that I love clothes, especially miniskirts. I was on a date with a Mr. Maybe when he complimented me on my miniskirt but added, "Could you please not wear that again because I don't want other guys looking at you?" Oh, hell no! He was not going to tell me how to dress! My response? "I am 26 years old and nobody tells me how to dress." His response? Silence. He said absolutely nothing. Remember, I decided in the second grade that didn't want a controlling man.

"The relationship you have with yourself sets the foundation for the relationship you have with others."

— Unknown

16 Dating Suggestions

When searching for employment, you send your resume to several employers, right? It's not wise to send one resume and hope you are called for an interview before applying for another job. If you apply for one job at a time, you risk being unemployed longer or not at all. Searching for your life partner is no different.

Earlier I advised you to get to know him before you even consider thinking of engagement. The second-best advice is to date as many men as possible. Do not stop at the first man who resembles your Man Plan requirements. Date lots of men. In other words, don't put all your eggs in one basket. Give yourself several opportunities to compare the men to one another. This will build your self-confidence and you will be more discerning about men. Ultimately, you will fine tune your Man Plan and be more certain of what you want. You also won't be sitting around waiting for that one guy to call, wondering if you're his Ms. Right and if the relationship is going somewhere. Take control and don't be passive. Expose yourself to a wide spectrum of men. Believe me, you'll take less crap from any of them. See yourself as the prize. Not him.

Start interviewing as many men as possible. This is not about a quick hookup but your search for your life partner. He has a huge role to play in your life and you want the best candidate. How are you meeting men? Are you waiting for them to approach you at grocery stores and gas stations? Are you going to singles' meet-ups or speed-dating events? Are you using online dating sites that have a big pool of the men you want to meet?

Think very strategically about where you're going to show up if you want the right man to find you. Adjust your online dating site settings so that you show up in the daily matches of the men you desire. Forget about being passive. That doesn't get you what you want. You are not the prey. You are the prize so take control. Get their attention and make the first move and say hello first.

The First Date

Make it quick and simple ~ one hour. In one hour you will know if you want to invest in a second date. You may not think one hour is long enough, but it is. Meet in the middle of the day at a coffee shop or right after work for happy hour and let him know in advance that you have other plans after your date. This way if you find that you don't like him enough to plan a second date, you've wasted little time, can chalk it up as a learning experience, and you already have an excuse not to stay longer. Should you really like the guy and want that second date, you'll leave wanting him more and leave him wanting more of you.

After the First Date

Repeat: DO NOT start your quest for Mr. Right by dating only one man in hopes that he is THE ONE! Too often women will commit to one man before they even know him. What a time waster! When you zero in on just one man, you're more likely to focus on the good and avoid acknowledging his warts. Let's be honest. Everyone has good qualities and those qualities shine bright in the beginning of the relationship. He is presenting his best side and so are you. When you date a few men at a time, you are more likely to eliminate the ones with the most warts without giving it much thought. Dating volumes of men you could have a first date, a second date, and a tenth date with three different men in the same week. In that same week, you may discard one or two of them because you've decided they aren't measuring up to your Man Plan after all because the others are looking better. Date volumes of men before committing to a serious relationship.

Online Dating

This is a great opportunity to interview several men. Dissect their online profiles. Remember, it only takes a split second to know if you are attracted to him. Keep the initial communication short and set up your first date. You don't need to spend several days or weeks corresponding before meeting in person. If you delay meeting in person, you'll start fantasizing about who he might be, only to realize later that he's nothing like your fantasy. Don't waste your time being delusional. Set up several dates with several men. There's nothing wrong with this. They're doing the same thing. Read more about online dating advice on the last page of this chapter.

The Setup

Let your friends know you are available and ready to date. Ask them if they know someone who may be a good candidate. Your friends know you. Your friends have friends. They'll be happy to set you up.

Work

Many women have met their husbands at work or through work. Look around. You may already know him.

Place of Worship

The single men stand out. They are not hard to find. If he has a wife, she'll be right there by his side.

Dating Clubs

You'll meet men who are also actively looking for a date. Check your city for dating clubs. Some clubs offer Speed Dating nights which are a lot of fun and you won't be held hostage by a bad date since each "date" only lasts a few minutes and then you're onto the next candidate.

Sports & Fitness Clubs

If you are into sports and fitness, look for like-minded men. Whether it's Crossfit, racket ball, cycling, running, there is a club with men.

Friends & Family

Ask your friends and family to be on the lookout for someone to introduce to you. Don't miss this opportunity. Just tell them you have a Man Plan now.

Online Dating Advice

BEFORE YOU BEGIN

◊ Mentally prepare yourself to meeting strangers
◊ Sign up for free versions of several sites
◊ Be open to dating many people at once

YOUR PROFILE

◊ Create a profile that is informative and concise
◊ Include several photos
◊ Be honest about yourself
◊ Check your spelling and grammar
◊ Ask friends to review your profile for feedback
◊ Do not use photo filters or Photoshop your photos to look better than you really are.
◊ Check the background of your photos (no piles of dirty dishes or laundry)

COMMUNICATING

◊ First contact should be short and to the point
◊ Accept rejection; not everyone will be attracted to you
◊ Schedule the first date sooner rather than later

BE CAREFUL

◊ Let someone know where you will meet your date
◊ Be aware of online dating scams - if they ask you for money, BLOCK THEM!

About the Author

Denise DeNicolo holds a master's degree in Counseling & Human Services from the State University of New York at Oswego. She has extensive experience as a therapist and program manager in various settings in non-profit agencies, residential treatment centers, and military facilities. Denise has a full-time independent practice in Bulverde, Texas, providing a wide range of services to diverse populations.

Denise is passionate about helping her clients with relationship issues, offering advice about dating, marriage, family relationships, self-fulfillment, and encourages independence and self-respect.

Prior to settling in Texas, Denise lived an unpredictable, yet exciting life as a military spouse until her husband retired with 30 years of service in the US Army. She is an "Army Brat" and also served four years active duty in the US Army.

Denise is not one to sit still for long, as she has many interests and hobbies. She is a marathon runner, enjoys sewing, crocheting, making wine, refinishing furniture, collecting antiques, refurbishing old houses, and selling real estate. Yes, and she still makes time for friends and family too.

www.ingramcontent.com/pod-product-compliance
Lightning Source LLC
Chambersburg PA
CBHW041959150426
43194CB00002B/68